disc

21st Century Junior Library

FARM ANIMALS
PIGS

by Cecilia Minden

CHERRY LAKE PUBLISHING * ANN ARBOR, MICHIGAN

Published in the United States of America by Cherry Lake Publishing
Ann Arbor, Michigan
www.cherrylakepublishing.com

Content Adviser: Laurie Rincker, Assistant Professor of Agriculture, Eastern Kentucky University

Photo Credits: Cover and page 4, ©iStockphoto.com/idizimage; cover and page 6, ©iStockphoto.com/chrisbence; page 8, ©maigi, used under license from Shutterstock, Inc.; page 10, ©charles taylor, used under license from Shutterstock, Inc.; page 12, ©Sergei Didyk, used under license from Shutterstock, Inc.; page 14, ©Joel Calheiros, used under license from Shutterstock, Inc.; page 16, ©iStockphoto.com/RollingEarth; cover and page 18, ©Ankevanwyk/Dreamstime.com; cover and page 20, ©Nancy Gill, used under license from Shutterstock, Inc.

LIBRARY OF CONGRESS CATALOGING-IN-PUBLICATION DATA
Minden, Cecilia.
  Farm animals: Pigs / by Cecilia Minden.
    p. cm.—(21st century junior library)
  Includes bibliographical references and index.
  ISBN-13: 978-1-60279-542-6
  ISBN-10: 1-60279-542-8
  1. Swine—Juvenile literature. I. Title. II. Title: Pigs. III. Series.
  SF395.5.M56 2010
  636.4—dc22   2009003676

Cherry Lake Publishing would like to acknowledge the work of
The Partnership for 21st Century Skills.
Please visit www.21stcenturyskills.org for more information.

CONTENTS

Pigs may surprise you!

Who Says Oink?

Have you ever seen cartoons about pigs? How do they act? Are they lazy and dirty? Maybe they do not seem very smart. That might be true for some cartoon pigs. But real ones are different! Pigs are some of the smartest animals on the farm. Let's learn the facts about pigs.

Piglets drink their mother's milk before they are weaned.

These Little Piggies

A **sow** gives birth to **litters**. There might be 10 or more **piglets** in a litter. Imagine having 9 brothers and sisters!

Piglets weigh about 3 pounds (1.4 kilograms). They stay with their mother until they are **weaned**. Then they move to the nursery, where they eat grains.

Pigs will eat bugs and worms that they find when rooting.

Pigs are **omnivores**. They eat meat and plants. Pigs like to **root** with their **snouts**. They use their snouts to dig for food in the ground.

Pigs are also clean animals. They like to sleep on clean, dry straw.

Think!

Do you sweat during gym class? Pigs cannot sweat enough to cool off. Pigs can even get sunburned! Think about it. Why might pigs roll in mud on a hot day? Hint: Have you ever stuck your feet in mud? How did it feel?

Farmers around the world sell their pigs at markets. This farmer is taking his pigs to a market in Cambodia.

Young pigs are sometimes called **shoats**. Shoats weigh more than 100 pounds (45 kg). They live in places called grow-finish barns. They stay there until they are 5 or 6 months old. At that age, they can weigh more than 230 pounds (104 kg)! Then it is time for the pigs to go to market. Some females and **boars** are kept for **breeding**.

Pork is prepared in many different ways.

To Market, To Market

Pigs are sent to packing plants. There the pigs become the meat you see in stores.

The meat from pigs is called pork. Pork roasts and pork chops are two forms of pork. Some pork is made into bacon or sausage.

Leather is very strong. It can last a long time.

Leather can be made from the skin of a pig. This leather is used to make different things. Sometimes gloves and belts are made with pigskin. It is also used to make furniture covers.

Ask Questions!

Do you know anyone who does not eat pork? Is he or she a family member or close friend? Ask questions! Ask this person why he does not eat this meat. People who practice certain religions do not eat pork.

Feral swine are good at finding ways to survive.

Hog Wild

Not all pigs live on farms. Some wild pigs are called **feral swine**. Feral swine can live in many different places. Some live in deep forests. They usually stay where they can find food and water.

Did you know that pigs make many sounds? They talk to each other by making different sounds.

Pigs like to stick together.

Pigs are smart. Some people believe that pigs are smarter than dogs. Being smart helps pigs survive in the wild. They take care of each other's piglets. They work together to find food and stay safe.

Pigs also have a sharp memory. They remember where food can be found.

Have you ever seen pigs on a farm?

Now you know more about pigs. They are smart and clean! They give us many things.

Cartoons about pigs are funny. But aren't real pigs more interesting? They are amazing farm animals!

Make a Guess!

Guess how much an adult boar weighs. How about a sow? Write down your guesses. Do you think males and females weigh the same amount? You might be able to find the answers online. Other books about pigs might help, too.

GLOSSARY

boars (BORZ) male pigs

breeding (BREED-eeng) mating and producing piglets or other young

feral swine (FEE-ruhl SWINE) wild pigs

litters (LIT-urz) groups of certain baby animals born to the same mother at the same time

omnivores (OM-nuh-vorz) animals that eat both meat and plants

piglets (PIG-letss) baby pigs

root (ROOT) to dig or turn over soil

shoats (SHOHTSS) young pigs

snouts (SNOUTSS) the noses of pigs

sow (SOU) an adult female pig

weaned (WEEND) switched to eating solid foods instead of drinking milk from an animal's mother

FIND OUT MORE

BOOKS

Ling, Mary. *Pig*. New York: DK Publishing, 2007.

Ray, Hannah. *Pigs*. New York: Crabtree Publishing, 2008.

WEB SITES

Fort Wayne Children's Zoo—Domestic Pig

www.kidszoo.org/animals/Pig.htm
Learn more about pigs

National Pork Board— Pork 4 Kids

www.pork4kids.com/Visit.aspx#
For links to a young farmer's journal and a slide show about life on a pig farm

INDEX

ABOUT THE AUTHOR

Cecilia Minden, PhD, is a literacy consultant and author of many books for children. She lives with her family near Chapel Hill, North Carolina. Cecilia was eight years old when she saw her first live pig. It was at her Aunt Catherine's farm in Arkansas. It was a very big pig!